Rude Insults Every Man Should Know

Jason S. Jones

Naughty Adult Joke Book

Dirty, Slutty, Funny Jokes That Broke The Censors

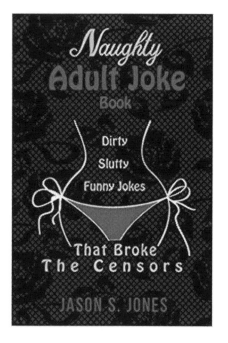

Why is a vagina similar to bad weather?

Once it wets, you have to go in.

https://www.amazon.com/dp/1793146985/

from various sources. Please consult a licensed professional before attempting any techniques outlined in this book.

By reading this document, the reader agrees that under no circumstances is the author responsible for any losses, direct or indirect, that are incurred as a result of the use of information contained within this document, including, but not limited to, errors, omissions, or inaccuracies.

Table of Contents

INTRODUCTION..7

CHAPTER 1: A REALITY CHECK 12

GENERIC..13
FOOD AND DRINK 23
SPORT..32
MUSIC AND DRAMA 38
MOVIES AND TELEVISION 45

CHAPTER 2: A PERSONAL AFFRONT! 51

WOMEN AND MEN..51
AGE 55
RACE 63

CHAPTER 3: INSULTS FROM THE BEYOND 71

HUMANITY..71
GOD AND RELIGION 78
MORALITY..85

CHAPTER 4: GLOBAL WARFARE..96

NATIONS 96
PLACES..107
PEOPLE, POLITICIANS, AND GOVERNMENT 113
LEFT AND RIGHT 119

CHAPTER 5: WORK HAZARDS 126

WORK 126
JOURNALISM..136

Writers, Publishers, and Critics 141

Doctors and Psychologists..144

Law and Lawyers...147

CONCLUSION **150**

REFERENCES..**153**

Introduction

You need to know a few insults.

Sometimes, the best response is a quick retort that should leave your listener speechless. You should be able to say, "Your Mama is so bald, you can read her mind" and end the conversation right there. You are probably wondering why I am encouraging you to equip yourself with insults. Let me explain with a little scenario:

Imagine a castle with a fairly large gate. Guarding the gate is a soldier equipped with a large sword. Now that you are aware that the guard has a deadly blade, can you automatically label the guard as a criminal? Can you identify him as a horrible person or someone with evil intent merely for having a weapon to defend himself? If bandits were to one day try to attack the castle, is it not necessary for the guard to have a weapon to send the impudent bandits scurrying off?

In your case, your insults represent your large sword. The castle is your pride, self-respect, character, and dignity. The bandits represent the people who take it upon themselves to attack you without rhyme or reason. Despite your best attempts to avoid conflicts or be nice to everyone, some people simply push the wrong buttons. Now it is understandable if the person does not know much about you and accidentally does something that you might find uncomfortable or offensive. For example, let us assume that you know someone who likes to clap someone's back every time he or she cracks a joke. He or she might be unaware of the discomfort they are causing you. They think that you are okay with the claps. In such cases, a polite request would suffice. You might probably get the person to stop clapping your back entirely.

However, when push comes to shove, you might need a few verbal weapons of mass destruction to drop some hurt bombs on a few people who deserve it. Of course, I would never recommend you to pick fights. But a few strategically placed snarky insults might just be the thing you are looking for that will also showcase your quick wit and sharp brain.

One of the questions that people often ask is: When did people started insulting each other? I would place a safe bet on the "since the time man became aware" moment. I bet that during those times—since language wasn't yet introduced in civilization—a few quick growls and hollers would have left someone's pride in minuscule pieces. These days, growls and hollers might get you raised eyebrows and people questioning your overall sanity.

There is no precise record of when people started insulting each other. If you peel back the curtains of history, then you might find insults dating back to the 1500s. During those years, you never had the 'variety' that you now possess when you would like to insult someone. Some of the words they used back then were tame by comparison. Insults such as 'simpleton,' 'dunderhead,' and 'nincompoop' were actually considered extremely offensive. Shakespeare used them liberally in his book, however, and they all took aim at a person's intelligence. It was simple yet effective. Why? It is because, ever since those days, people have already taken pride in their intellect. Why else would they have so many of the greatest writers in history packed into one time period, from

Shakespeare to Machiavelli to Swift? Let's just say that 'blockhead' was to the 1500s what 'sh*thead' is to the 20th century.

Yet the insults of the 1500s are presently used by little people below the age of 12. In fact, if you, as an adult, would walk up to a person with determination in your eyes and ready to destroy his or her pride with a verbal assault, only to utter a mere 'nincompoop' word, then you might just get a chuckle out of him or her. So much has changed in our vocabulary. You could say that, while language evolved, so did the way we could insult other people.

Insults are a reflection of our times. They are meant to attack the ideas, values, styles, and personalities that we consider important to modern times. That is why insults went from targeting mainly a person's intelligence to using colorful ways to insult mothers through the ever-popular "Yo Mama" jokes.

And it is into this modern time that we take a step into and discover a plethora of verbal bombs that are just waiting for you to dispense at your worst enemies.

Before we begin to assault a person directly, let us look into generic cuss words and insults that target certain interests.

Chapter 1: A Reality Check

People love to have a supply of generic insults. Let's call these phrases the 'classics.' They are the insults that you know very well. They are the 'kiss my arse' to 'screw you' phrases. And that's where we are going to start today. But, that being said, we aren't exactly going to simply say 'go to hell' or 'shut your trap.' Nay, my reader! We are going to display some sick burns that should be an essential part of your vocabulary.

Generic

Meeting People

I envy the people who haven't met you.

Living Children

Just out of curiosity: Do your parents have any children that lived?

Never Underestimate

I am trying to underestimate you, but you make it impossible.

Dumb and Dumber

You are not the dumbest person on this planet, but, for your sake, you better hope he/she doesn't die.

And the Trophy Goes To...

If you were an inanimate object, you would definitely be a participation trophy.

Dumb and Prettier

I wish you were pretty enough to justify how dumb you are.

A Matter of Priorities

I want you to take my lowest priority. Then, I would like you to place yourself below it and leave me alone.

Shitness Protection

I wonder if your ass gets tired of the shit that comes out of your mouth.

Light Em' Up

You are so dense that light just bends around you.

Sperm Donor

I still wonder how you became the sperm that won.

Marriage Proposal

I do hope your future husband/wife brings a date to the wedding.

Hereditary Skips

If the genius skill skips a generation, then I know your children will be brilliant.

Rotten Charm

You have all the charisma and charm of a rotting corpse.

Colorful Crayons

I wish I had enough time and crayons to explain this to someone of your intellect.

Being Understanding

I can explain it to you. But I can't understand it for you.

Coming To An Agreement

I would love to agree with you, but then we would both be wrong.

Nice Place

What's a girl like you doing in a nice place like this?

Whitewashing

You are as important to me right now as a white crayon.

Pigeon Breasts

You are as important to me right now as breasts on a pigeon.

Talk of the Town

Now I know why people talk about you only after you leave.

Chromosomal

Don't make me hit that extra chromosome out of you.

A Cold Spot

Wear some underwear/panties next time. Your ankles are pale with cold.

Just Passing By

Your IQ and the life expectancy of the average man recently passed each other in opposite directions.

A Good Gargle

Some people drink from the fountain of knowledge. It appears that you just gargled.

Speak Out

Don't hesitate to speak your mind. You have nothing to lose.

Twice For Half

I think you need twice the brains to qualify as a half-wit.

Sleep Time

You don't need beauty sleep. You need to hibernate.

Brains, Not Brawns

You are definitely as strong as an ox. And also as intelligent as one.

Leaving Early

Do you have to leave so soon? I was about to poison your drink.

Oxygen Deprivation

Ever wondered what life would have been like if you had enough oxygen at birth?

Respectfully Accepted

When I think about people I respect, you are definitely there—serving them drinks, that is.

Chin Up!

Hey, there is something on your chin. The third one down.

Big Assets!

If people ever tell you that you are an asset, tell them they are off by two letters.

Looks Are Everything

Do you always feel the way you look?

Stretching It

You are so fat, your car has stretch marks.

Example of a Warning

It is okay if you cannot be a good example. You can be a horrible warning after all.

Wee Hours

How was the sex? Thanks to you, it now hurts when I wee.

Food and Drink

Don't like someone's food habits or cooking? Want to show your distaste for food in a clever and snarky way? With the below insults, you are going to lay down a barrage of offensive word combinations, the likes of which the listener might not have expected.

It's Oysteresting

I don't want to eat these oysters. I want my food dead, not wounded and sick.

Cracking The McDonald's Code

Going to McDonald's for food? That makes as much sense as visiting a crack house for vitamins.

Cafe Prison

Visiting this cafe for coffee is like going to prison for sex. You know you are going to get it but it's most definitely going to be rough.

Horsing Around

This looks like horseshit. And I don't mean that metaphorically.

Oil Content

There is more oil in this dish than all the fields in the Middle East.

Fishy Business

This fish is so undercooked, it's still looking for Nemo.

A Vet Lamb

This meat looks so alive that I can take it to a vet.

Eat Meat

This dish is the reason I don't want to be a vegetarian.

A MATter of Lasagna

Is this lasagna or a doormat?

Black Food Matters

This food is so black, it has its own record label.

Seasonal Food

This dish has the same amount of seasons as the bloody moon.

Ratting It Out

I'm sorry, but I don't have a pet rat to feed this to.

Dietary Restrictions

I said I wanted to go on a diet, not commit suicide.

INSULT TIP: You can turn this to reflect numerous situations. Some examples are:

- I said I wanted to eat dinner, not commit suicide.
- I said I wanted to eat fish, not commit suicide.

Confining the Chef

You could become a chef. In solitary confinement.

Menu Options

Do you have anything with flavor on this menu?

It's Smokin'!

This chicken is so smoked, it needs an oncologist.

Birthday Surprise

Hi, yes. I ordered food about an hour ago. Any chance it's going to come before my 90th birthday?

Taking a Piss

Adding pineapples on this pizza is like taking a piss in the fuel tank. The car might still work, but I don't want to find out.

INSULT NOTE: Get creative with this one. Talk about any ingredient that is added to a particular dish.

Rationing Food

The Army's food rations taste better than this sh*t.

Cooking Recommendation

Have you tried, maybe, cooking it first?

Feed the Hungry

There are hungry children around the world. I think they would rather thank their situation than eat this.

Alcohol Content

This drink has barely enough alcohol to fight an infection.

INSULT NOTE: On the flipside, you could even say:

This drink has enough alcohol to kill the Ebola virus.

The Horrors of Food

This should be in a horror movie.

The Scope of the Food

I would rather get a colonoscopy than eat this thing.

Garbage Disposal

You cook food and throw garbage. Not the other way around.

Fitness Regime

I entered what you had fed me into my fitness app and it sent an ambulance to my house.

Amazon Delivery

No thanks. I'd rather order bacon and eggs from eBay.

Cavemen Food

The last time you put this thing into the fridge, the cavemen discovered fire.

Sport

Do you want to insult your favorite sport? Or maybe you would like to throw an insult at a player while watching your favorite sport? Try these insults.

Ballin'

Pass the ball, not travel with it. You're playing basketball, not discovering a new continent.

Family of Players

Are you sure you are the best player in your family?

Slow Paced

He/she is so slow, he/she would finish third in a race with a pregnant woman.

A Certain Skillset

He/she cannot kick the ball well. He/she cannot pass, and he/she cannot score a goal. He/she can do anything else other than play the game.

Million Dollar Baby

Why should someone pay this player a million dollars to play when they could pay $5 to a 10-year-old and get him to play better?

Game Time

I am not saying that this game is bad, but if I were to prepare a stew with my eyes closed, it would come out better than this crap.

Name of the Game

I wonder if he/she can spell their name better than they play ball.

INSULT TIP: Simply replace the word 'ball' with your favorite game, and you can turn this insult to any sport.

Octopus Fuss

Think of an octopus with wings. Not possible right? Now think of your sporting talent.

Ballers

Practice with your balls. I meant those things between your legs because you are never coming close to a football ever again.

Killing the Sport

If I wanted to kill myself, I would climb your so-called sporting talent and jump to your incompetency.

Watering Down

You mean you are not the water boy?

INSULT TIP: You can replace 'water boy' with any other title, depending on the sport. For example, if you are watching or playing basketball, you could say:

You mean you are not the cheerleader?

Bad Sport

I don't think you are bad at this sport. I just think you are someone who should be shot and buried for attempting to play it.

INSULT TIP: You can use this to talk about any player playing any sport. All you have to do is replace "this sport" with the actual sport. For example:

I don't think you are bad at baseball. I just think you are someone who should be shot and buried for attempting to play it.

Clap Trap

People clap when they see you play. They clap their hands over their eyes.

Sports Land

In the land of talentless sportspeople, you would be king/queen.

Sporting Genes

Your sporting talent is the reason the gene pool needs a lifeguard.

Getting Far

Someday, you will go far in sports, and I hope you stay there.

Music and Drama

Don't like your favorite band? Or perhaps that drama at the local theatre was so horrible, you wish you could delete your memory of that play. Let's take a look at some insults you can use to express your feelings about music and drama.

Love for Drama

The best part of the play? How about the part after the end?

Instrumental Skills

Your piano skills? I think you're better off shoveling snow.

Sing Like a Goose

He/she sounded like a goose being strangled.

Confidence Boost

I have the utmost confidence that whatever play you will be part of, you will single-handedly ruin it for everyone.

Meditative

I'm sorry, that was not a meditation session for sleep disorders?

Work Motivation

Avoiding watching you play music is the perfect excuse for getting stuff done at work today.

Highway Accident

Your talent must have been born on a highway, because that is where most accidents happen.

A Trick That Works

I don't know what makes you so talentless, but it's working so well.

Talent is Everything

Talent isn't everything. In your case, it is nothing.

Animalism

I would slap you for being a sh*tty actor/actress, but that would be animal abuse.

Relaxing Moment

After watching that play, I feel like doing something relaxing. Like going into a coma.

From Bad to Worse

You are not as bad as people think. You are much worse.

Acting Talent

There is no vaccine against your shoddy acting skills.

Pool Diving

Watching this drama is like jumping naked into a pool full of hungry sharks.

Case File

That guitar should file a restraining order against you.

INSULT TIP: Simply replace 'guitar' with your favorite musical instrument, and you will be throwing verbal daggers at someone's skills in no time!

Licensing Problems

Don't you need a license to be that talentless?

Crime and Punishment

Being a horrible drama is not a crime, so, sadly, we can't take it to court.

Bear Tussle

If it's between fighting an angry bear and watching this horrendous drama, I'd choose to fight the bear. Without weapons.

Alien Invasion

Ah, you must be new to our planet. Let me show you how to play that.

Spotting Mistakes

You can always tell when you are about to make a mistake. Just watch yourself play.

INSULT TIP: You can replace 'play' with 'act' or any other action that represents the world of entertainment, music, and the arts.

Galaxy Quest

1 galaxy, 8 planets, 7 continents, 190-plus countries, 7-plus billion people, a trillion combinations of events, and I had the misfortune of listening to you play.

INSULT TIP: You can use the above insult for numerous results. Don't like someone's speech?

1 galaxy, 8 planets, 7 continents, 190-plus countries, 7-plus billion people, a trillion combinations of events, and I had the misfortune of listening to your speech.

Don't like a movie?

1 galaxy, 8 planets, 7 continents, 190-plus countries, 7-plus billion people, a trillion combinations of events, and I had the misfortune of watching this crappy movie.

Movies and Television

Some movies or TV series are so bad that you just wish you could articulate your displeasure at watching them, right after wondering how you are going to get the lost time back. Fortunately, we have a slew of insults for your communication purposes.

First and Last Date

This is supposed to be a romantic movie. But I had taken someone to watch it on our first date and he/she liked it... There won't be a second date.

The Good, the Bad, and the Ugly

There are good movies. There are bad movies. There are ugly movies. And then there is trash. And finally, there is this movie.

Bad Taste

Some movies/TV shows leave a bad taste in your mouth. This one gave me a full-on halitosis.

Airsickness

Watching the contents of an occupied airsick bag is more interesting than watching this movie/TV show.

With a Passion

Flies have shown more passion when attempting to sit on food than the actors have shown passion with each other in this romantic movie.

Credits Roll

The most interesting part of the movie/TV show was the credits.

Lamp Light

The lamp in the background had more acting skills than him/her.

Dead to Rights

You should never say bad things about the dead. Because that's what this movie is. Dead.

Brain Dead

I don't think there was a single brain behind the making of this movie.

International Borders

This foreign film was terrible. Absolutely terrible. It is the reason why the US borders should be more secure.

Fire Hazard

This film is so wooden, it's a fire risk.

Factory Produce

Did they make this movie at the stupid factory?

So Unique

This movie/TV show is marginally better than the worst movie I've ever watched. But that's like saying that suffocation is marginally better than drowning.

I See Dead People

The actors/actresses in this movie look like they died 3 years ago and no one bothered to tell them.

Chicken Flick

This movie is supposed to be a chick flick. The writers fed the script to chickens, collected the resulting sh*t that came out, and ran it through a camera.

Oh, The Horror!

It was a horror movie alright. Just awfully horrifying.

The Jokester

I recollect some knock-knock jokes in my head during the more unfunny parts of this comedy movie, which was practically the entire movie.

Friends Forever

My friend Jacob told me to watch this. Jacob is no longer my friend.

INSULT TIP: Replace Jacob with the name of your friend, acquaintance, or any person to create an impact for the insult.

Chapter 2: A Personal Affront!

Targeting someone's gender or personal characteristics is like aiming for the heart with a bazooka. Not only will the impact not miss, but it will utterly demolish the person. Fair warning; use it only on those people who deserve it. You know what they say about great power and it having great responsibility.

Insult responsibly.

With that, let's move on.

Women and Men

Sometimes, you just target the person's gender when they are looking to make fun of yours. Be careful where you use some of these insults, as some situations might draw a large mob, and you don't want to be in the middle of that.

For Her

- You have your whole life to be a bitch. Why not take a break today?
- Did your parents wish for a son and you came out as an accident?
- The only place you have any degree of depth in is your cleavage.
- You look like you put on your makeup during an earthquake.
- The only woman you can compare yourself to is the 'before' part in a 'before and after' photo.
- How will your face look after sixty? Well, open a map and look at the landmass of Ireland.
- If you are going to be two-faced, can you at least make one of them pretty?
- I love what you have done with your hair. How does it flow out of your nostrils like that?
- The only way you are going to get laid with makeup like that is if you crawl up

a chicken's ass and wait.
- If I truly wanted a bitch in my life, I would have gotten a dog.
- Jesus loves you. Everyone else, however, thinks you are a bitch.
- You are a good combination of beauty and brains. That is, a lack of beauty, and if you were engaged in a battle of wits, you would be unarmed.
- You are fighting for women's empowerment? Shouldn't you be supporting endangered species?
- You are as useful as a vibrator with no batteries.

For Him

- Hey. Your village called and they want their idiot back.
- I would love to slap you but that won't make you any better.
- Just because you have one between your legs doesn't mean you have to be one.
- Your family tree could be a cactus since you are such a prick.

- What are you doing all the way out here? Did someone leave the cage open?
- We all evolved from apes but it seems like you did not evolve enough.
- The only dates you are going to get are the ones on a calendar.
- Please stop talking. You are never going to be the man that your mother is.
- Perhaps you might need some makeup.
- Behind every ugly man, there is a handsome man. No, seriously, you are in the way.
- I would say that you are funny, but, sadly, looks are not everything.
- Someday, you might go far. Just stay there and don't come back.
- You aren't stupid. You just have bad luck when thinking.
- What's the difference between your boyfriend and a walrus? One smells of fish and has a mustache, while the other is a walrus.

Age

Want to show someone how old they are? Try doing it with a little wit. And offense, of course.

Archeology

Is your husband/wife an archaeologist? He/she must be taking a serious interest in you to stick around.

Prism Sight

Perhaps if I look through a prism, you might look younger.

Dust Buster

You look so old, you probably fart dust.

Jurassic Park

Does watching Jurassic Park bring back memories for you?

Raisin the Raisins

I don't know how to say this politely, but the back of your head looks like a raisin.

Commanding the Commandments

Did you co-author the Ten Commandments by any chance?

Biblical Proportions

I have a feeling you have a signed copy of the bible. Can I see it?

From Prince to King

Ah. You must have memories of the time when Burger King was still a young prince.

Oiled Up

Do you oil your joints in the morning?

Supper Time

Yo Mama is so old that she was a waitress at the Last Supper.

Antiquities

How do I put this lightly? If you were to enter an antique store, they're not going to let you leave.

Glyphs

I bet she has hieroglyphics in her driver's license.

Age and Death

If I told you to act your age, you might just die.

Birth Update

I have a feeling your birth certificate is expired.

Numbering the Age

Age is just a number. Yours is a mathematical anomaly.

Google Search

You must be proud that Google named their company after your age.

Time and Age

I could use your age to measure the time humans have spent on Earth.

Down Memory Lane

Are your memories in black and white?

Innovating With The Times

You are probably so old that your innovative idea went obsolete during the Stone Age.

History Class

Were there still history classes back when you were in school?

Dead Seasickness

I bet when you were in high school, the Dead Sea was just getting sick.

Pimp My Ride

How was it riding the chariot to school?

Party Friends

How was the Boston Tea Party? Made any friends back then?

Security First

You must be pretty old. I'm guessing your social security number has only a single digit.

Fossilized Remains

What's a fossil like you doing in a museum like this?

Reducing the Digits

I could divide your age by a hundred, and there would still be five digits remaining.

Ancient Wheelie

How was it witnessing the introduction of the wheel?

Checkout Prices

Will that be all? That will be five Aztec gold coins and three silvers, please.

Portrait Quality

There's a portrait of you. In cave art.

Race

There are many aspects to race—from the language to the culture. Let's look at how you can incorporate some comebacks and insults using those criteria.

An Act of Selfishness

It's a bit selfish of you to not speak English, don't you think?

Keeping the Pet

Where I come from, we take care of the family pet, not eat it.

Dieting Encouragement

Thanks to your local cuisine, I can finally get back on my diet.

Appreciating Beauty

We are all beautiful. Except you folks. You guys are full of sh*t.

Robbery in Motion

Here's 20 dollars. Please don't rob me.

Getting Good

I wish walking was an achievement. You guys would be good at something at least.

Roped In!

If you guys can have the rope free of charge, I bet you will let yourselves be hanged.

Extinction Level

More than 90 percent of all living things that have ever lived on Earth are now extinct. I guess Nature took pity on you guys.

Evolutionary Changes

If evolution was a tree, you people are still at the roots.

The Growth of Civilization

By the time you people become civilized, human beings would be space-faring creatures.

Putting Up For Adoption

Were you all adopted by the human race?

Are You Smarter Than a Human Being?

I bet when Nature was turning humans smarter, you people were the last in line.

Circumcising the Race

I bet I know why circumcision is popular in your race. Bet the ladies don't touch anything that isn't 15% off.

The Name Game

How do you people name your kids? Do you drop them down the stairs and see what sounds they make?

Racing To the Finish Line

Bet you people enjoy cross-country races a bit too much, don't you?

Soul Power

Does your complexion match the color of your soul?

The Stuff That Belongs

The only reason I would ever go to a garage sale held by you folks is to get my stuff back.

Tools and Equipment

I found your race under synonyms for antique tools.

Being Athletic

I bet that anyone who can jump, swim, or run among you people is already in the US.

Family Commitments

Guess what an elevator can do that you guys can't? Raise a family.

Nose for Air

I bet you guys have big noses because the air is free.

Test Subjects

Special thanks go to Nature's test subjects for the rest of the human race.

Inventions

Did you guys invent that or borrow it from someone else?

Creationism

God created the heavens and the Earth. The rest was probably made by you Chinese.

Animal Farm

Are you guys your country's national animal?

Chapter 3: Insults from The Beyond

This section might just enter an otherworldly realm, where we insult things that might not necessarily be a characteristic or a physical property. We are going to insult concepts.

Let's get right into it.

Humanity

Sometimes, it is good to make fun of the human race as a whole. We certainly are responsible for so much destruction, after all. So, what are the some of the wittiest ways to do it? Let's find out.

Looking Up At the Stars

As I looked up at the millions of stars out there, I realized just how useless we are.

STDs

Humanity itself is a rather fatal sexually transmitted disease.

Natural Selection

We are all fatally flawed. As far as natural selection is concerned, we are okay, and that's why we are here.

Fair Treatment

Expecting life to treat all humans fairly is like expecting a crocodile to not eat you because you are a vegetarian.

Aping Out

It's not difficult to see why we are often thought of as evolved from apes. Dolphins are cool. Giraffes are cool. Even hippos are cool. Apes are assh*les.

Flooding the Truth

God forgot to sink Noah and his family while he was flooding the entire Earth. Would have saved a lot of trouble, I assure you.

Alien Invasion

I bet aliens who are planning to invade us are looking through their scopes and saying, "No point in doing anything here. They f*cked themselves over pretty good."

Sperm Count

I think that human beings and sperm have a lot in common. They have a one-in-a-million chance of having a winner.

Being Unlucky

There are billions of planets in our galaxy, and Earth was unlucky to have us.

Robot Uprising

I'm sure robots will make good use of us in the future.

To Infinity And Beyond

The universe and human stupidity are both infinite. Too bad only the former can be disproved.

The Rule of Half

The average person is quite stupid. What's shocking is that, to reach that average, half of humans had to be stupider.

Death before Thinking

I think most people die before they even begin to think properly.

Checking the Ability

I feel like God overestimated human capabilities when he created them.

The Beginning

In the beginning, God created the heavens, the Earth, and two hell spawns to create billions of other hell spawns.

From People to Mankind

I can see the enormous progress mankind has made. People, on the other hand, are as immature as the day they evolved from their predecessors.

Hell on Earth

How do we know that this world isn't the hell of another planet?

Intelligent Life

Do you know how I know that there is intelligent life out there? They haven't contacted us.

Today in History

History is the sum total of all the things that could have been avoided. Take the evolution of human beings, for example.

Aim for The Stars

Human beings should aim for the stars. That's right. Earth would be glad we are gone.

God and Religion

Taking a shot at the almighty and his religious creations? Perhaps you might need to arm yourself with these insults of godly proportions.

Achievement

I don't think God is evil. He/she is just an underachiever.

Maggot Brain

Human beings are idiots. They can barely create a single maggot, but they can definitely create Gods like fast food chains.

Fly Away

God had so much wisdom that he created the fly. I just wish I knew why.

A Matter of Belief

You have the right to believe what you want. Others have the right to find it idiotic.

Disproving Something

If you ever want to prove something doesn't exist, don't choose evolution or gravity. They have too much evidence. However, God and religion on the other hand...

Proof of Existence

Oh, I'm sure there is proof for the existence of God and religion. They are called "euphemisms" and "exaggerations".

Kill Count

According to the Bible, God killed more than 2 million people, while Satan took the lives of only 10 people. I think we are following the wrong person here.

Asking For Forgiveness

When you want something, don't pray to God and ask him for it. It's not how he works. Steal the bike and ask for His forgiveness instead.

Science versus Religion

People use science to fly to the moon. People use religion to fly into buildings.

Praying For Delusions

If you are praying to God, it's called religion. If God answers, then you probably have schizophrenia.

Made in China

If God really made everything, he's probably Chinese.

No Show

Want to know the best way to teach kids about God? Gather them in a classroom and then don't show up at all.

Everywhere and Nowhere

If God is everywhere, I wonder what that filthy b*stard is doing in a strip joint.

Doctor versus God

I feel bad for surgeons. As soon as they perform life-saving surgery, it's so typical of religious people to say "Thank God" and take all the credit.

Mentally Ill

Religion is what we thought about before we could clearly diagnose mental illnesses.

Religious Difficulty

It's difficult to be religious when certain people are not yet struck by lightning.

The Special Child

If we are all the children of God, then why is Jesus so special?

Hope without Hope

It's ironic how religion gives hope to people in a world devastated by religion.

Blind Faith

I respect faith. But only doubt gets someone a proper education.

The Cure

I think the best cure for any religion is reading their own books.

Choosing Airlines

If God is your pilot, change airlines.

In His Image

God made us in his own image? I didn't know Salvador Dali was a God.

Morality

Things can be moral or amoral. But these insults definitely maintain a fine line between the two.

Things That Go Together

You and conscience are like a hairbrush and a swimming pool; they don't go well together.

Full of It

I can see why you did it. But I still think you are full of sh*t.

Initial Assessment

I will always remember the initial misconception I had about you. Those were the good times.

Coincidence

Any similarities between your morals and mine are purely coincidental.

Left to The Imagination

Hold on. I'm trying to imagine you with a conscience.

Taping the Conversation

Does everyone imagine a duct tape over your mouth when you speak?

Under a Microscope

Your morality is so insignificant, it cannot be found even under an electron microscope.

Blissful Existence

If ignorance is bliss, then you must be the happiest person alive.

Close Encounters

Don't stand too close to him/her. You can hear the screaming souls of hell.

The Journey

You have a conscience? Must have been a long and lonely journey for it to finally reach you.

Vaccinations

There is no vaccine against amorality.

The Emptiness Within

Do you ever have an empty feeling in your soul?

Waste of Creation

God wasted a good asshole when he put it in your personality.

Thinking about You

I couldn't stop thinking about you the whole day. I was reading about Hitler's amorality.

Talking Crap

I think you should teach your ass to talk. Much less sh*t might be exposed that way.

Calling the Tooth Fairy

Your conscience has a lot in common with the tooth fairy; it doesn't exist.

Time Limit

Go on, describe your conscience to me. I'll give you 10 seconds, but I'm afraid that's too much time.

Equal Rights

Don't say that everyone is your equal. People have better morals than you.

Live and Let Live

People have a lot to live and learn. You, on the other hand, just live.

Flush It Out

Your morals remind me of what I flushed down the toilet this morning.

Mind Shifts

You're changing your mind? And you think the new one will be any better?

Nature Calls

I would love to insult your brain, but I'm afraid I won't do as well as Nature did.

Self-Reflection

Well, hello there, you self-centered, shallow-minded douche machine. How can the world help revolve around your pitiful self today?

Breaking the Wall

Some babies were dropped on their heads, but you were clearly flung to the wall.

Speed of Light

Did you know that light travels faster than sound? It's why you look bright until you speak.

Making a Point

You are the jelly to my burger, the knife to my water, the cotton ball to my sushi, and the mayonnaise to my ice cream. My point is, you are completely pointless.

Lollipop Mind

Well, aren't you a fun little lollipop triple-dipped in a psychotic mind.

On The Inside

Maybe you should eat some makeup. You might get pretty on the inside, too.

Zombie Food

Zombies love brains. Just saying, because you are going to be perfectly safe in a zombie apocalypse.

Garbage Collector

Hey, just letting you know that the trash is getting picked up tomorrow. Be ready by then.

When All Is Said and Done

I am sorry I called you an amoral prick. I thought you already knew.

MRI From Hell

If I take an MRI of your brain, will I find Satan's handprint in there?

So Weird

I'm not weird. I'm just outside your exceptionally narrow view of the world.

Chapter 4: Global Warfare

It is time to take over the world.

We are going to target nations, places, people, and a lot of other things that make this world what it is.

Let's ease our way into a global warfare by starting with nations.

Nations

Want to insult a particular country? Many of these insults can be fine-tuned to attack any nation.

Sex Drive

I seem to have lost my sex drive since visiting your country.

Departing

I spent a week in the departure lounge before I finally got to your country. It was the best week of the holiday.

On The Right Track

Our trains back home smell nearly as bad as yours.

Shoe Troubles

It seems like I have some sh*t stuck under my shoe. Nevermind, it's just everything in your country.

Something Fishy

I must be near the sea. I smell the fish. Ah, it's your city's center.

Nice View

Wow, your country looks beautiful. My bad, I was looking at the sea.

Straight Answer

If the people of my country behaved like the people in your country, they would be put in straightjackets.

Clean Up

I think your coastlines could use a little cleaning up. Maybe a quick tsunami or two?

Import and Export

I think your country should export all its people to an abandoned island and import some intellectual people.

Between Two Nations

The only decent thing between our nations is the sea.

A Place Called Home

If this country were my home, I would seek asylum elsewhere.

From Peasants to Royal Family

This is fascinating. I haven't seen a country with so many peasants. Look, they are even part of your royal family.

Hairy Situation

In my country, it is not normal for people to have hair there.

Description Not Needed

I don't know how to describe your country. Is there a word stronger than "pathetic" and "ugly"?

Filling Up the Land

How do I find your country? Well, let's put it this way. Even the landfill site back home in my country has more wonderful geographical features than your country.

Leftovers

It's like Earth decided to create all the other nations first, and whatever useless chunk of land that was left became your country.

Educational Level

You guys have education in your country? I don't see anybody displaying an educational background here.

Space Face

I bet that looking at your country from space is like looking at a large and ugly mole on someone's face.

Firm Patriotism

Of course you guys are patriotic. Idiots are not welcome everywhere in the world.

Zoo Keeping

Your country is like a zoo with an incompetent zookeeper.

Car Control

I feel like your president is the driver of a fancy car and your people are the car's passengers. Your president has great control. Right up until he hits the tree.

Slogan Nation

I think your country's official slogan should be: "You came. You saw. You got slaughtered."

Movie Business

Let's face it. Nobody gave two cents about your country until we started making movies there.

Ancient Bankruptcy

I had hoped that having thousands of years of history might have saved you guys from bankruptcy.

The Value of Importance

You know, at one point, you guys were important. Now you are just good for making shoes.

INSULT TIP: Pick out the characteristic of a country and then replace 'shoes' with it. Let's say you would like to insult Amsterdam. You could say:

You know, at one point you guys were important. Now you are just good for having a red light district.

Money Bag

The only thing you guys are good for is taking someone else's money.

American Dream

I am not saying your country is the U.S., but you guys are trying so hard to be.

Terms of Surrender

If I had a dollar for every time you lost or surrendered in a war, I could get a decent meal for the entire month.

From Bad to Worse

I can't imagine things getting any worse in your country. Then again, I don't live in your country.

Places

What if you don't want to insult an entire country? What if you would like to target specific places? Let's see if we can do that here.

Sci-Fi

Reading about this place is like reading science-fiction. I reach the end and think: *There's no way that would happen.*

Books and Reality

It looks better in the books.

In The Room

I can make better discoveries in my room than in this place. And I have been in my room for 10 years.

INSULT TIP: You can change various parts of this insult. For example:

I can have more fun in my room than in this place. And I have been in my room for the past 2 months.

Shocking

This is what I call a culture shock. I am just shocked by the culture in this place.

Lake of Pee

Is this supposed to be a lake? It looks like a hundred elephants got together and took a piss.

Digging Deep

This was an archeological dig site? They should have kept it buried.

The Stuff of Paintings

This place looks like a painting. A painting that was drawn by a drunk, blind, and old man without any painting experience.

Two Places

There are two kinds of places: Those that are good, and those that aren't. This one is not even a place.

The Quality of the Building

It's just a building with walls and some fancy painting. And I had to pay to see this sh*t?!

Discovering Ruins

They said it was ancient ruins and that's what it was. It ruined my holiday.

Rock Steady

Far too expensive to simply look at a rock arrangement.

View from The Top

The view from my balcony is more majestic.

Towering Delight

The tower across the street is way better.

The Future is Here

Futuristic my ass! Minimalism doesn't always equal the future. It shows laziness.

Inside Out

The outside is as bad as the inside.

Rating High

It's overrated. I am surprised that it wasn't demolished and the parts weren't used to build something else—maybe a dozen more houses for the people.

Beer Preference

My recommendation is that you see it from afar, take a picture, and go have a beer nearby.

Magnetic Energy

It's just a tourist magnet and nothing else. Even then, it attracts the wrong crowd.

People, Politicians, and Government

Trying to make sense of politics and governmental laws can be quite daunting. But you can definitely make it easier with these comebacks and insults.

Freedom

On a scale of North Korea to America, how free is your country right now?

Show of Hands

I think we should get rid of democracy. All those in favor, raise your hand.

Voting For Diapers

Politicians and diapers have one thing in common. They should both be changed regularly, and for the same reason.

General Consensus

It is true that 100% of your people think that at least 50% of your people are mad.

Stealing Balls

You know what's the difference between politics in your country and baseball? In baseball, you're out if you're caught stealing.

Myth and Legends

You know what's my favorite mythical creature? It's an honest politician.

INSULT TIP: You could even talk about the government or people this way. Here are a couple of examples:

You know what's my favorite mythical entity? A government that supports its people.

You know what's my favorite mythical story? It's about people who vote for the right person.

Looking For Trouble

Politics is the fine art of looking for trouble, finding it, misdiagnosing it, and then applying the wrong remedies.

Caught Stealing

You don't have to steal. It's our government's job.

Communist Much?

Your government's ideas are like communism; everyone is supposed to get an equal share, but it's only ever good in theory.

Horror Time

Remember when watching *The Exorcist* on TV was considered scary? Now it's our government on the news.

Repeating

Imagine that you are an idiot. Now, imagine that you are a member of the congress. Wait—I think I just repeated myself.

Serious Comedy

It's funny how people are taking comedians seriously and view politicians as a joke.

Epic Fantasy

In another world, the government would be just and the people smart. Like, maybe in the pages of a fantasy novel.

Lord of the Rings

Is there a ring I can throw in a volcano and destroy this politician? No? Thought I'd ask.

Swearing Curses

He/she got sworn in, but I can't wait for him/her to get cursed out.

Left and Right

Sometimes, it is difficult to pick sides. And then there are other times when you wonder if the other person even made the correct decision. Here's how you let them know.

Likeness is Uncanny

Everyone is born alike, except the left and the right.

Liberal Fights

A liberal person is one who leaves the room when a fight breaks out.

Confusion

You don't have to try too hard to confuse a liberal. They are born that way.

Elvis Has Left the Building

I think I have figured out the difference between Elvis and a smart liberal. Elvis had existed.

Muggings

A liberal is just a conservative that hasn't been mugged yet.

Hold That Thought

You should hold your hands over your ears. That way, you can keep your liberal thoughts inside.

Rear-Ending

I can only tell you one difference between you liberals and the rear end of a horse: There really isn't one.

City of Spells

You liberals should stay in L.A. It's the only city you can spell, anyways.

The Rat Race

I'm telling you, when there is a liberal politician about to run congress, it's like watching a mouse become a rat.

Handicapped

Oh, you are a liberal? You should come with me to the supermarket. I can park in the handicap zone.

In For a Penny

I would like to give a penny for your liberal thoughts. I might just get the change.

Grandma's Help

You are a conservative? Do you still ask your grandma for advice on changes to be made to this country?

Thinking Stupid

I think you only get credit for being a conservative when you are stupid.

Finders Keepers

I think you conservatives think you deserve to keep the things you have stolen.

The Thinking Game

You know what I think about conservatives? They sit and think. Well, mostly just sit.

Walk on Two Legs

I like how you conservatives are like people with two feet who haven't figured out how to walk.

Opposition

Every time I think about conservatives, I think about people who oppose the things they are in favor of.

Organizational Structure

I think you conservatives would be good in office. No, truly. It's like organized hypocrisy. It would be an interesting social experiment.

Chapter 5: Work Hazards

Who loves work? Well, if you are happy where you work, then I truly am glad you found a place where you are comfortable. It is not often that people can say that. But if you find yourself at a workplace that you despise or you know of certain people who truly do not know how to do their jobs, then you might need to express your distaste and problems through some rather scathing remarks.

Fortunately for you, we are going through a list of them.

Work

Don't like your own work? Or do you have something to say to a co-worker? Perhaps these insults might help.

Law of Equals

Why is there a law that says that the one who does the least work gets the most credit?

Interruptions

Please don't say that you can't do it while I am actually doing it.

Taking a Leave

Have you ever considered taking a leave from the company? Like, permanently?

Getting a Drink

Oh, I was just getting some water to drink. It wasn't an invitation for you to talk to me at all.

INSULT TIP: You can change the above insult to fit a lot of situations. For example:

Oh, I was just getting a smoke break. It wasn't an invitation for you to talk to me at all.

Timely Emails

I got your email. It's just you that I don't get.

Leftover Problem

Are those the leftovers you said your wife makes for you? Boy, how bad are things at home?

Good Service

You spent how much on that service? Oh, wow. That's incredible! No, I mean it's incredible you thought I'd give a f*ck.

INSULT TIP: You can get creative with this one in so many ways.

You spent how much for that diet? Oh, wow. That's incredible! No, I mean it's incredible you thought I'd give a f*ck.

You spent how much on a new suit? Oh, wow. That's incredible! No, I mean it's incredible you thought I'd give a f*ck.

Happiness is Subjective

Oh, you guys are going to Happy Hour? That's great. No thanks, I already have a happy hour every day. It's the hour that I spend heading home and where I don't have to listen to you guys anymore.

Elevator Company

Don't get me wrong. You are a nice person, but just because we are in the same elevator, doesn't mean I want to talk to you.

The Jokester

That is a nice joke! Are you a comedian on the side? Do you do a 9-to-5 and jump into a stand-up routine at the local bar?

Presenting Stuff

Your presentation was perfect. I just have one question about all the slides from the first to the last.

Invitation Only

I am so sorry for not responding to your baby shower invite. It's just that I find it hard to remember responding to someone I don't give a sh*t about.

Weekend is Here

I hope you have a great weekend. And I am only saying that because I have nothing else nice to say about you.

Tying it Up Nicely

Your tie is a little askew. But so is your personality.

Suit Up

You wearing a suit to look smarter is like McDonald's thinking it's fine Italian cuisine.

Team Building

We are going to have team building activities? Can I have a team for "I don't give a f*ck?"

Helping Hand

You are as helpful as a blister on my fingers.

Working Together

I can't really think of you as a co-worker if you haven't done any work.

Seeing the Future

You know where I see myself in this company in three years? Probably gone.

Working on Principle

Why was I not working? I didn't see you come in.

The Average IQ

After working with all of you guys, it makes me wonder if people are all just dumb, or if I am just smarter.

Speaking To Someone

I'm confused. Do you want to speak to my manager, or to someone who knows what's going on?

High Five

You need a high five. In the face. With a chair.

Job Waiting

I don't mind going to work. But the eight-hour wait to go home is just ridiculous.

Tolerant Speech

I get along with people just fine. I just find it hard to tolerate idiots.

Firing Squad

I wonder how you get away with doing things that I would get fired for.

Being an Ass

You have kissed the manager's ass so much, I
can smell his/her fart on your breath.

Journalism

Think journalists have no ethics these days? Or perhaps you haven't looked too fondly at the way journalists cover news? Well, you have these insults to express yourself well.

Literary Writing

I think journalism is literature written in a hurry by a bunch of ape brains.

The Mighty Pen

The pen is mightier than the sword. Just not in your hands.

INSULT TIP: You can use the insult for any other journalist. For example:

The pen is mightier than the sword. Just not in his/her hands.

Smarty Pants

He/she wants to look like a smartass. Trouble is, you have to be smart first, otherwise, you are just an ass.

I Got 99 Problems

99 percent of journalists give the rest a bad name.

Vocabulary

A journalist is just a writer with limited vocabulary.

Undoing the Past

I think journalists need a CTRL Z in their life. Just to undo the fact that they became journalists.

Learning the Language

That journalist needs to learn a new language: English.

INSULT TIP: You can target this insult to a journalist who speaks your language. For example, if you were watching the news and listening to a Spanish journalist, then you can say:

That journalist needs to learn a new language: Spanish.

The Right Condition

This journalist looks like he/she has a condition. Hopefully, it's something serious to justify his/her journalism.

Dulling Things

That journalist is not just dull, he/she is the reason for dullness in others.

Support Structure

That journalist uses words the way a drunk uses a lamp post—as a support instead of making a point.

Reporting Stuff

He/she looks less like a reporter and more like they should be part of the report.

Filling up Forms

If I wanted this reporter's opinion, I would ask him/her to fill out forms.

Ad Placement

Is this the news or an advertisement for mental health awareness?

Writers, Publishers, and Critics

How can you insult writers, publishers, and critics? With sharp wit and a sharper tongue.

Papers Please!

Think of the trees that were cut down to make paper for his/her lack of talent.

Publishing Rights

If Moses were alive today, he'd come down from the mountain with the Ten Commandments and spend the next five years trying to get them published.

Squaring Things Off

All that you are, you owe to your parents. Why don't you send them a penny and square the account?

Childhood Dreams

I don't think I have ever met anybody who said, "When I grow up, I wanna be a critic."

Scouting Talents

What incredible writing skills! You can probably make a career out of writing the epitaph on a tombstone.

Driving

I am sure that the critic is at his/her wit's end. He/she didn't have far to go.

Balancing Things

Everything should be balanced. For every great writer, there is a sh*tty publisher.

Picking Things

I would like to pick your writer's brain for a minute. Can you tell me where it is right now?

Critical State

Don't feel bad. A lot of critics don't have talent.

Doctors and Psychologists

You have to respect doctors and psychologists. And sometimes, you just want to insult them. Here is a list of insults for that.

Degree of Intellect

Did you really need a degree to be that stupid?

Wrong Diagnosis

Tell me, have you ever treated yourself?

Explaining Things

Can you do me a favor, Doc? Pretend you are talking to a smart person and see if you can explain it to me better.

Scientific Results

There is a medical condition for what you are, Doctor. It's called being an idiot.

Naming Ceremony

Just because you have a name for the condition doesn't mean you have explained everything, you smart ass.

Trust Issues

You see, I don't really visit a psychologist because I have trust issues with morons.

A Cure for the Cure

I don't think you have cured anyone, Doctor. People have just left in disgust.

Accentuating the Problem

As a psychologist, you seem to have the same problem as me. You just have a different accent.

Charging the Right Fee

You studied medicine but you charge me like a real estate agent.

Law and Lawyers

Some people protect the law, and some people do a terrible job at it. And some laws are meant to help you, while others seem to make fun of you. Which is why you have the below insults to express yourself better.

Charge!

The only difference between you and a herd of buffalos is that they charge less.

Morgue Lawyer

If I wanted to find a good lawyer, I'd visit the city morgue.

Shark Tales

I wish I could throw you in shark-infested waters, but they might not eat you out of professional courtesy.

Trustworthy Partner

It's not that I don't trust you as a lawyer. It's just that, if I was stranded on an island with you, Adolph Hitler, and Attila the Hun, and I had a gun with two bullets, I would shoot you twice.

Liar Lawyer

I can tell that you are lying. Your lips are moving.

Snake Law

The only reason God made snakes before lawyers is so that he could practice perfecting his creation.

Law Jokes

I like reading about the law. They have such funny anecdotes.

Siding with the Law

The law is definitely on my side. The other side has a poor bank balance.

Conclusion

One of the best things about insults is that you can change one to fit another scenario. Sure, some of the insults are classified under a heading, but that does not mean that you cannot use them in creative ways for many purposes.

You could use some of the lawyer jokes on people you don't necessarily trust, and so on.

But with all things said and done, remember not to use insults liberally. Intelligent and wise is not the person who has witty comebacks and smart insults, but the person who knows how to use them well. You might definitely find yourself at a moment when you have to launch your verbal assault, and at those times, ask yourself:

- Is it really worth it?
- Can I not resolve this situation without exacerbating it further?
- Do I really need to insult this person?

Finally, remember that insults should be used in defense. Never provoke someone, even if you think they deserve it. Be wise. Be smart. And most importantly, be ready to open a can of what I would call a "verbal whoop-ass."

Naughty Adult Joke Book

Dirty, Slutty, Funny Jokes That Broke The Censors

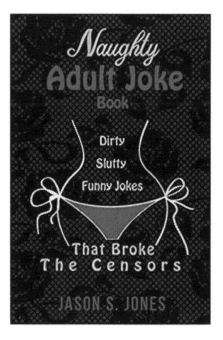

Why is a vagina similar to bad weather?

Once it wets, you have to go in.

https://www.amazon.com/dp/1793146985/

References

McPhee, N. (1978). *The book of insults, ancient & modern.* New York: Paddington Press.

Safian, L. (1997). *The giant book of insults.* Secaucus, N.J.: Citadel Press.

Printed in Great Britain
by Amazon